A Beautiful Life

Life

- Life needs to be lived, not just to be passed -

Sachin Gupta

Printed in India by
Manipal Technologies Limited

ISBN: 978-93-5776-285-4

First Printing, 2023

The Write Order

Koramangala, Bangalore

Karnataka-560029

THE WRITE ORDER PUBLICATIONS.

www.thewriteorder.com

Translated by Gautam Choubey and Santosh Soni
Formatted by Ranjana Dubey

Dedication

I dedicate the book 'A Beautiful Life' to my parents, every member of my family, my wife Sanyokita, my son Gaurik (Sach) and all my friends. This book is meant for all those facing troubles in real life or looking for a competent guide to help them make a particular decision. This book will be handy for those who have made wrong decisions and are now looking for ways to set them right.

From my parents, I have learnt to do hard work and not to do or think ill of others. My maternal grandfather Late Shri Parmanand Motele Ji, has taught me always to follow the path of altruism. I have learnt how to lead a good life, to live with honour and self-respect from Omprakash Gupta Ji, who was fondly called Chacha Ji by one and sundry, and the art of being a good administrator from Dr. Rajesh Bhargava, who is currently the Registrar (Academic) at Rajiv Gandhi Proudyogiki Vishwavidyalaya, Bhopal. I have learnt the attributes of good values, Gau Seva or the service of the cows, to be soft-spoken, caring for all and involved in social service from my elder paternal uncle, Shri Laxmi Prasad Kinker Ji. He has written several books which are soon to be published, and it was he who inspired me to take up writing.

He has devoted himself to the service of the cows and is a good poet as well. Hailing from a rural background and having studied and *served in various fields, I have understood the finer aspects of life in detail. I dedicate this book to all those who have cooperated directly and indirectly in writing this book and thank all those because of whom this book saw the light of the day and reached its readers.*

Sachin (Sach)

Sachin has always made us proud with his achievements and also by being an obedient son and a great human being. He has made us even more proud by writing a book that will contribute to adding value to the lives of people. Our blessings are always with him.

-Shambhoo Dayal Gupta and Sudha Gupta
(Parents)

With the grace of Gaumata and the blessings of Guruji, I wish that other renowned literary personalities come forward and shower their blessings on Sachin for this beautiful endeavour in making people's lives better with this book.

-Laxmi Prasad Gupta 'Kinkar'
(Tauji)

You have succeeded in reflecting on the fundamental ideas of how to lead a good life in easy-to-understand language by keeping the core idea concise and to the point.

Dr. Virendra Kumar
Union Minister of Social Justice and Empowerment
Government of India

It is a manual for joyful living. Today, we are surrounded by technology of all sorts, and one must successfully learn how to use it to one's advantage for better work-life balance and live in harmony with one's purpose.

Omprakash Sakhlecha
Cabinet Minister
Department of Micro, Small and Medium Enterprises and
Science and Technology
Madhya Pradesh Government

The author has presented the story of his life's ups and downs and created a living manual for the readers who can use this template to work around their life's problems with the author's experiences, offering them viable solutions.

Dr. Pramod Kumar Agarwal,
Senior IAS (Retd.)
Author of 70 books

While reading this book, readers will relate with their life and past experiences.

Dr. Shefali D. Jain

This book can help you lead a simple, sweet, interesting, exciting and delightful life. It is the social code of conduct on how to lead a successful life.

Padam Singh
Film Actor and Producer

The book will prove a source of inspiration for many people. The author has skillfully woven the realities and experiences of his life and given us a book to remember.

Shailbala A. Martin (I.A.S.)

The book tugs at the heartstrings. The author has offered practical advice to keep readers in good stead throughout their lives.

Sheelendra Singh (I.A.S)

This book is an amazing effort in the direction where one gets the solution of the problems to live a better life while being in joyful state of mind.

Resham Dwivedi
(I.R.S)

This book expresses various aspects of life with great ease and teaches the virtues of striking a balance, the importance of decision making and living life cheerfully.

Harshal Choudhary
Deputy Collector
(Topper MPPSC-2018)

About the Book

"We have come to live life, not to spend it, so live every moment to your heart's content."

The book, A Beautiful Life, is meant for people of all ages and across all stages or roles of one's life, whether one is a man or woman, son or daughter, brother or sister, husband or wife, grandfather or grandmother, maternal grandfather or grandmother, among others.

As its name suggests, this book teaches the art of living. True to its title, this book will inspire people to live life to the fullest. This book is important for all people, be it a child learning the nuances of life and living or a person entering their twilight years.

Usually, people are good writers, good artists, good actors, good politicians, good businessmen, good executives, good managers, and good orators. Still, despite being competent in everything, only a few practise what they preach or say. I can confidently affirm that whatever has been written in this book is true in words and spirit. I have lived through them every moment. After reading this book, your way of thinking and living will undergo a drastic change, and for good; you will all be able to live a beautiful life and spend every moment of it in absolute joy.

I have found that nowadays, bookish knowledge is served everywhere, and sermons are given in the name of sanskaras (values). Apart from bookish knowledge, being aware of everything a person faces in real life is real education. Because mostly we see that the most influential politicians, big administrative officers, businessmen, agewise whether younger or older, happen to fall prey to a monster called depression and take the extreme step of ending one's life, quite unfortunately. These people are successful, but deep within, they are vulnerable. They cannot handle the ups and downs because they are always taught to be an achiever and succeed but never how to handle defeat or take failure in their stride. It is a mammoth miss that has serious repercussions for a person.

It is true to a tee that there is hardly any creature in the world who has not had to taste success and failure in equal measure. Everyone gets joy and misery in their lives, but one needs to handle both situations. This book is an effort in this same direction. It is a guidebook that prepares people to deal with challenges of all shapes and sizes and a way to counter them. It gives a template of courage and strength to face adversity and teaches how to live a beautiful life even in the most stressful times.

To be happy, it is not necessary to be successful in life because you can be happy even after a failure.

Sachin (Sach)

About the Author

"A successful person is one who is a good person."

Sachin Gupta, the author of A Beautiful Life, was born on Teacher's Day in 1987 in the family of a teacher in Chhatarpur district, Madhya Pradesh.

Sachin cracked Madhya Pradesh Public Service Commission (MPPSC) in 2014 and is currently posted as Chief Executive Officer in the Panchayat and Rural Development Department in Madhya Pradesh Government. But he started his career as a teacher. He took up a lecturer job in an engineering college before joining as an assistant engineer at Bharat Heavy Electricals Limited (BHEL). He cleared the Prelims and Mains and appeared for an interview for the Engineering Services Examination of the Union Public Service Commission (UPSC). He even sat for the Civil Services Examination before being selected for MPPSC.

Regarding his early years and academic pursuits, Sachin says, "I completed my education up to Class 10 living in a rural atmosphere, and after that, I did my diploma in engineering from Naugaon Polytechnic College and engineering from

Oriental College, Bhopal. I also got an opportunity to teach engineering students for almost a year. After this, I prepared for the Engineering Services Examination (ESE) from MADE EASY, a prestigious institute in Delhi. While preparing, I passed the GATE exam twice. I passed the examinations of several Maharatnas and Navratnas, Miniratna PSUs like BHEL, the Airport Authority of India, etc. I later appeared for UPSC exams, where I cleared the written (Mains) of the Engineering Services Examination. I faced the interview of UPSC twice."

I served in Delhi and Bhopal as an Assistant Engineer in Maharatna company BHEL for about six years. While working at BHEL, I prepared for the Civil Services Examination from Delhi's prestigious institute, Vajiram and Ravi. On not being selected in the Civil Services Exam conducted by UPSC, I appeared in the MP PSC exam. After being selected in MPPSC 2014 as a Chief Executive Officer, I currently serve in the Panchayat and Rural Development Department of the Madhya Pradesh Government.

Sachin firmly believes that problems come and leave us rattled, but they do pass without teaching us something or the other. The book, A Beautiful Life, will help readers learn the art of leading a good life, and, in some measure, it will also help them solve the problems they encounter in their lives. If it fails to solve the issues, it will help one to keep the chin up and deal with them patiently.Whatever is written in this book is completely based on true incidents and reflects the author's lived experiences. The author has followed whatever is written in this book and lived his life according to it.

All that has been mentioned in this book are actual and factual; nothing is fictional. While writing the book, ample effort has been made to ensure whatever is written in this book is original and not copied from any other book. An attempt has been made to explain the facts by changing the names and places of a few people so that their identity is protected and no one should have any problem with it later.

Therefore, there is no intention of hurting any person or any particular group, so if any person or group happens to relate the subject matter of this book to their personal life, then it will be just a coincidence.

Table of Contents

1. Goal

What is a goal?

Why is a goal necessary?

How to set a goal?

How to achieve a goal?

Abraham Lincoln failed 14 times and later became the President of America.

"If you are born poor, it is not your fault, but if you die poor, it is your fault."

-Bill Gates

Mostly the questions that arise in a person's mind are- What is a goal? Why should there be a goal? How to set a goal? etc.

Important information about the goal-

1. What is a goal?

2. Why is a goal important, or why is it important to set a goal?

3. How to set a goal or what should be a goal?

4. How to achieve a goal?

1. What is a goal?

Usually, people don't define the goal and, as a result, complicate the goal, whereas the word goal is simple. Without mincing words, I will explain it in a line. In simple language, a goal means what you desire or want, whatever you want to do or whatever you want to be. That is your goal.

For example-

My dream is to become an IAS officer. Here, the goal is to become an IAS officer.

I want to become a doctor. Here, the goal is to become a doctor.

I want to marry a nice girl. Here, the goal is to marry a nice girl.

2. Why is a goal important, or why is it important to set a goal?

Generally, most of the time, people need help understanding what they want in life or what they should do. Every person must think about their life and what they must do or how to live. When someone becomes a little older or, say, from the time they become sensible, they should clearly understand how they want to live their life from then on till their last breath. They should strive to make this their life's goal.

"If you want to do or become something, set the goal first."

-Bill Gates

Bill Gates, the co-founder of Microsoft, the world's largest software company, has said that setting a goal is the first step to making any work successful.

"Setting a goal is the first step in turning the invisible into the visible."

-Tony Robbins

The famous American writer Tony Robbins has said that before doing any task, one should set a goal because by setting a goal, the first step to seeing any impossible task that you cannot see is determined.

Setting a goal is also important to be aware of one's destination. For example, a person stands in a queue to get a ticket before the ticket window at the railway station but does not know where to go. When that person decides his destination and says he wants to go to Delhi, he takes a ticket to Delhi and travels in a Delhi-bound train. Similarly, when we set a goal, we know where and by which train to travel.

3. How to set a goal, or what should be the goal?

I do not say that every person should set a big and great goal. A person can make his life meaningful even by setting small goals. Not every person needs to set a goal to become the President, Prime Minister, businessman, actor, scientist, etc.

The objective of setting a goal for you should only be to learn how to live your life. Some people do not know what to do because they have not found any guide in the true sense. About

70 per cent of the youth in India cannot use their talent properly due to a lack of proper guidance and keep repenting after the time is gone.

Some important points to remember while setting a goal:

● The goal should be very clear.

● The goal should be achievable. While setting a goal, a person should know his/her abilities completely.

● While setting goals, both positive and negative aspects should be taken into consideration seriously.

Such as, if an Indian citizen sets his goal to become the President of America, then the goal setting starts on the wrong note because in order to become the President of America, first of all, it is necessary to be its citizen. Similarly, a person often sets a wrong goal and later gets disappointed when he fails to achieve it. Mostly a person is unaware of his/her goal, due to which he remains in trouble throughout his life. Certainly, ignorance is not bliss.

I will share a small example related to my own life:

An acquaintance younger than me, a boy who must have been about 22 then, ran away from his home and came to meet me. He said, "I am leaving home. I have not had any happiness at home; they all do as they wish, none cares about me, and now I will live my life on my own terms." As soon as he said that he was leaving home, I asked him where he was planning to go. The boy responded, "I will go anywhere but will not stay at home any longer." I asked him again, "Where are you going, and what will you do for a living?" He started thinking. He did not have an answer to this question. Then I persuaded him, saying, "Until you know where to go and what to do, you should stay back at home." Perhaps the boy realised that he lacked a goal and returned to home. Today the same boy is doing a good job and is happy.

One should set small goals instead of big ones to do something big in life, live well, and achieve an objective.

4. How to achieve a goal?

There are a few things to keep in mind while achieving the goal.

Your Health

Your Family

Your Economic Status

Your Social Responsibility

Your Health:

When you are on the way to achieve your goal, you should take care of your health because your goal lasts only as long as your health is good.

Your Family:

When you are on the way to achieve your goal, you also have to consider whether you can take care of your family. Whether you are going to stay home or have to be away from home. Being head of the family, your responsibility should be to maintain constant contact with the family, give time to your family, and discharge the duties towards your family members well. It is usually seen that a person happens to forget his body and his family to fulfil his dreams.

Your Economic Status:

While setting your goal, you should keep your financial status in mind.

Social Environment:

Any negative atmosphere should not be created in society duringachieving your goals. You should always bear this in mind.

Achieving your goal does not mean giving up what you are

currently doing. Having a goal helps in setting priorities in the tasks going on simultaneously in life. Such as, we take a bath every day, eat food, do all our daily routine tasks, and when we set a goal, we also devote time daily to achieve it. Because in today's fast-paced life, one has no option but to multitask. To pursue a goal, we work by choosing those options in conformity with the goal.

When you set a goal, you work towards fulfilling it. It also makes you aware of the challenges and opportunities to achieve the goal. So all human beings need to have a goal in life.

I will share my own example:

I had dreamt of becoming a great engineer since childhood. I still needed to know who an engineer is, what he does and what one has to do to become an engineer. Whatever strong desire one cherishes, nature takes them from him in that very direction. As a child, I had a strong desire to become an engineer. Therefore, I became an engineer, but I could not become a big or great engineer as after becoming an engineer, I understood that this was not my goal. In fact, by then, I had hopped on to another goal.

One's goals keep changing according to time. And these changes should continue because the age of attaining maturity varies from person to person. But at a certain age, or say by 21, you should know your goal or what to do. After becoming an engineer, I realized that I wanted to become an IAS officer, but when I was not selected for IAS, I understood that nature had made me do something else, and my goal changed. I understood that I have to become a good person because a good person has all the qualities that a successful person has.

Practice

What is the goal of your life?

What efforts are you making to achieve the goal?

----

2. Education

Education leads to an all-round development of the human being.

Education (study) never goes in vain.

A change can be brought in society through education.

Education supports you throughout your life.

"Education is the weapon with which you can change the world."

-Nelson Mandela

Nelson Mandela, the great leader of the world, has said that with the help of education, you can change the world.

"A life full of joy and happiness is possible only based on knowledge and science."

-Dr. Sarvepalli Radhakrishnan

Dr. Sarvepallavi Radhakrishnan, the second President of India and a lifelong teacher, has said that a life full of joy and happiness is possible only based on knowledge and science.

Nowadays, everyone wants to give good education to their children and wants their child to become an officer, businessman, leader, actor, doctor, scientist, engineer, etc., after completing their studies. It is the wish of all parents that, like their unfulfilled dreams, children's dreams should not remain unfulfilled, so they sacrifice their comforts and put efforts day in and day out into shaping their children's future.

Despite making all efforts, several times it happens that the child fails to get a job as per the parents' expectation, and then both the children and the parent get disappointed. Still, providing education should not mean that if the child fails to get a job or is unable to earn well, or is unable to do anything worthwhile, then education proves abortive.

With the help of an example, I will tell you how education leads to the overall development of a human being and how education is useful everywhere.

A confectioner lived well by running a sweetmeat shop, but he always thought his son should do a good job instead of running a sweetmeat shop like him. He cared for the education of his child, who was good in studies too from the very beginning. The confectioner's son topped the entire district in Class 12 and later studied abroad.

After studying abroad, he got a good job there with an annual package of about ₹25-30 lakhs. Things were going well. Here in India, his father ran the shop and sold sweetmeats worth around ₹10-15 thousand per day. Once when his father's health worsened, he called his son, "Son, I am no longer capable of minding the shop and will have to either shut or sell it." Hearing this, the son said, "Father, I came here only to study, to learn new things and to see the world, so my purpose is fulfilled. Now I have to return to India."

He convinced his father, saying, "Father, your shop has been a reputed one, and you have worked very hard for this, and now it is my responsibility to take care of you and develop your business further. Now I am coming back."

The boy returned home and shouldered all responsibilities of his family. He gave a new look to the shop and did good management; consequently, the daily sales grew from ₹10-15 thousand income per day to ₹25-30 thousand. This sale of ₹25 to 30 thousand brought a profit of about ₹10-15 thousand per day. While living with his parents, he took good care of them and gave a new dimension to his family business.

Through this example, I just want to say that whatever is there in one's possession, one should realize its value and act accordingly. In the example, this boy made a good decision because his father was alone at his home. This is what I mean to say that the meaning of education is what newness you can bring in yourself, in your family, in your business or in your society. If all these things are put together and seen, then things are possible only when you study well. Education never goes in vain, it makes you learn something or the other, and it is of great use throughout your life.

Practice

What are the benefits of education obtained by you and your family?

Make a list of positive aspects of your life due to education.

----

3. How to be happy?

What is happiness, or what it means to be happy?

Why should a person be happy?

What does a person generally do to be happy?

What should a person do to be happy?

"The purpose of our life is to be happy."

-Dalai Lama

The great Tibetan spiritual leader, the Dalai Lama, has said that our life's purpose is happiness. If we are not happy in our life then, all the achievements of the world are useless.

Before knowing how to be happy, we need to know some things:

1. What is happiness, or what is it to be happy?

2. Why should a person be happy?

3. What does a person generally do to be happy?

4. What should a person do to be happy?

1. What is happiness, or what is it to be happy?

When a smile or a feeling of happiness comes on your face, even for just a moment for any reason, and then you forget everything and become joyful, it is called happiness.

One does not need to do much to be happy. It is very easy to be happy. Big classes are organized at several places to be happy; people consult a doctor, attend motivational classes, read many books, go to temples, mosques, gurudwaras, and churches and consult spiritual or religious gurus of their respective faiths. But even after doing everything, happiness seems far away from them, and in the true sense, it can be said that they do not know how to be happy.

Being happy depends on one's own nature. To be happy, one should find happiness in small things.

For example, if a person is unhappy and has a husband, wife, mother, father, son, daughter, etc., at home, he can only be happy in his family. Let me give a simple example: every human being or every living thing likes to eat, and if a person gets the food of one's choice, then everything else takes a backseat. The person becomes happy for the time being. If a person is sad or disappointed, the simplest way to cheer them up is to let them eat their favourite food. By eating the food of one's choice, that person gets happiness for some time and happens to forget all the miseries.

To be happy, a person should act according to his wishes. For example, if a person feels like going to a pond, playing badminton, listening to music, dancing, etc., he should act accordingly. One should act according to one's hobby as it gives instant pleasure to a person.

One thing that most people have forgotten these days is entertainment. Entertainment is a medium to be happy. A person should always retain that child in one's being. A child is innocent and carefree. Even the small joys of life bring a lot of happiness to the child, and that's one quality to notice. One should not think that a person who holds a big office, is a big leader or is too old or young cannot enjoy little pleasures of life, including a peal of hearty laughter. One should stop worrying about what people will think of you if you guffaw. What others will think is entirely their prerogative, so there is no point pondering over it much. Above all, one should always remember that being happy brings joy to others in the immediate surrounding, encompassing one's family, friends, and distant ones, including society. Happiness is contagious. If it spreads, it brings more happiness.

The other thing that one needs to be mindful of is that one's happiness is a standalone subject and shouldn't depend on others. Often the cause of a person's sadness or happiness is another person, be it the family, friends, relatives or others in society. But one's happiness shouldn't hinge on others. One should be happy on one's own.

2. Why should a person be happy?

"If you are not happy, then life has no significance."

-Osho

Acharya Rajneesh Osho Ji has also said that if you are not happy in your life, then your precious life is of no value.

"If you haven't laughed in a day, that day is in vain for you."

-Charlie Chaplin

The great English comedian Charlie Chaplin has even gone to the extent that if you spend a day of your life without laughing, that day is completely useless.

"My pain may be a reason for somebody's laugh. But my laugh must never be the reason for somebody's pain."

-Charlie Chaplin

The great English comedian Charlie Chaplin said that if he feels pain and that pain brings a smile to someone's face, he likes that pain too. He has also said that if someone is hurt or offended due to his laughter, then that laughter is meaningless.

Today everyone is engrossed in fulfilling one's duties and responsibilities so much that one has almost forgotten to be happy. I ask you whether being happy is so tough? Is being happy a pipe dream?

The profound thoughts of these well-known personalities show that being happy is the reason for our being and living to seek happiness, big or small, whenever and wherever possible.

That's why I say:

Being happy lies in everyone's hands.

Being happy is no less than being successful.

Everyone has the right to be happy, and happiness is everywhere.

Do or don't do something, but at least be happy and spread joy.

Being happy is the solution to all problems.

Every person should look for reasons to be happy, come what may.

3. What does a person generally do to be happy?

Pay attention to these points to know what a person does to be happy:

He seeks happiness outside.

He enjoys being at parties with friends.

He goes to watch a movie.

He spends time with a girl/boy.

It is clear that man wanders here and there in search of happiness and keeps looking for happiness outside his home while happiness lies around him. Something is hidden within him, which he does not even try to search for. All you have to do is to find your happiness within yourself.

Nowadays, some people have interlinked success with happiness. These people believe that there are many problems in life and there are many responsibilities, so how can one be happy? Some people consider being successful as a synonym for happiness. For those who think that success begets happiness, it is not necessary to be successful in life to be happy; it is possible to be happy even after facing failure.

4. What should a person do to be happy?

This question is often asked- How should one be happy?

The first thing is that you should not compare yourself with anyone.

One should not be happy or unhappy because of others.

Happiness is present all around you.

One should find happiness in small things.

A person never stumbles on big mountains or rocks. He stumbles only on small pebbles or small things lying on the path. Similarly, happiness comes from small things, and it does not require big opportunities or great achievements.

A pleasant atmosphere should be created at home.

It is the responsibility of everyone- mother, father, husband, wife, children and youth- to ensure a happy atmosphere at home.

Sometimes, you can be happy even after losing.

Sometimes, you can be happy even by being called a fool.

You can be happy by doing whatever you like.

If you feel like listening to songs, playing a game or eating something, and you do so at that time, you will instantly become happy.

Try to live in the present:

People usually get worried, thinking about their future or feeling afraid of past mistakes. Living in that past makes one worry unnecessarily; it fosters stress and worry. If you have to remember old things or times, reminisce only the good ones and retain only those that make you happy.

Some people think that living is all about whiling away one's life as if it is a task. Spending an uneventful day, just waiting for it to get over, seems like an arduous achievement. To such people, I would like to say that"we have come here to live life, and to the fullest, not just to spend it somehow."

So live every moment of life to the fullest and be happy. It may neither come back again nor would you be able to revisit that lost moment ever.

At any time, you can be content and happy:

When I completed my engineering degree and did not get placed in any company, it began to seem that nothing was in my hands. I was staring at a bleak future and did not know what I would do thereon. Such a thought occurred not as much in my mind as others dumped it.

There was always a feeling of satisfaction in my mind that I had at least studied engineering. Some people don't even get a chance to go to school or college. I considered my education as my most significant privilege. I thought that I had completed my education. I repeatedly thanked God, my parents and everyone else who at least made me complete my studies. My degree became my stepping stone and gave me the confidence to achieve everything.

When the result of my Engineer Services Examination (ESE) was announced, I was shattered. I failed to clear the competitive exam by a few marks. Those lost marks made me sad, but at that very moment, I realized that I am currently working with BHEL, and it is a dream job for many people. I am not unemployed despite not being selected, and I became happy within no time. This acceptance gave me peace and a sense of satisfaction that gave way to happiness.

This is how happiness is present around us, within us. We just need to find it. However big disappointment may be there, it brings along a ray of hidden hope that is always lurking around it. One just needs to make an effort to let it flow in full glory.

You can be happy even in the most difficult situations or in the face of failure. So happiness is pretty much in one's hands.

Practice

Are you happy in your life? If not, why?

What are the things that nature has given you to be happy?

----

4. A person who changes your whole life

There is nothing else to change your life.

You have to write your destiny.

You should trust your hard work most.

A person who changes your whole life, who is he?

"The stars in the sky are not powerful enough to decide our life, but the decision of our destiny lies in our hands."

-William Shakespeare

Renowned English playwright William Shakespeare has said that a man should write his destiny, none other than the actions of a man that can decide one's fate.

"A man who can neither speak nor walk but can shake the whole world with the power of his thoughts, then why not you?"

-Stephen William Hawking

You all must have heard about the great British physicist Stephen William Hawking. Stephen Hawking was diagnosed with Amyotrophic Lateral Sclerosis (ALS), which hindered his speech and mobility. No part of Hawking's body worked except his brain. He could neither speak nor walk nor do any work himself, but despite all this, he used his mind and had the whole world shaken by the power of his ideas. He researched space and time and proved to be a great physicist.

Hawking believed in himself and made the world accept his worth on his own. Once, the doctors had told Mr Hawking that he would live hardly for two years, but Mr Hawking proved all the doctors' claims to be false due to his positive bent of mind, and he went on to live for 50 more years with ALS.

The person who changed the life of Hawking was none other than himself.

"Know for sure that none other than yourself can bring you success."

-Napoleon Hill

Napoleon Hill, a great American author, wrote several books and said in one of his books that a person should not depend on anyone else to be successful. Still, one should achieve success by trusting oneself based on hard work because none other than you can ever bring success.

"I don't believe in failure. If you have enjoyed achieving success, then it is not failure."

-Oprah Winfrey

You must have heard the name Oprah Winfrey, one of the world's most influential women today, but looking at her past, you won't believe how she single-handedly changed her life's course for good. Winfrey's early life had been quite a struggle. She underwent the trauma of being raped at the tender age of nine, and she got pregnant at 14, and her baby died while still in the womb. Despite all this, Winfrey did not give in to the crises and completed high school at 19. Despite all the hardships, she made the world accept her talent based on her hard work and unending self-confidence. She became a source of inspiration for women worldwide and proved that a woman is competent to make any impossible task possible.

I have found that some people always cherish the illusion that someone will happen to come and will change their whole life. As a girl cherishes a dream from her childhood that when she grows up, a charming prince will come her way and marry her. That prince will love her, always keep her happy, fulfil all her wishes, and change her whole life. After his arrival, all her troubles will vanish.

Similarly, a boy thinks that a dream girl will appear in his life whom he will marry. That dream girl will love him a lot, will always keep him happy, and will feed him well after her arrival; his whole life will undergo a sea change.

This hardly happens in real life. It happens in dreams only because someone or the other comes into everyone's life, and as mentioned above, favourable things are likely to happen with some people. Still, with most people, when it does not happen then, they get disappointed. And finally, you find that a person who can change your whole life is none other than you, so always know yourself and make decisions about your life according to your desire and ability.

Practice

Who is going to change your life?

Can anybody else do your work?

Can any person always be with you in every trouble?

Mention all the works (good or bad) which you did yourself.

----

5. Real joy of life

The real joy of life is nowhere else but in the present.

Every human being should live in the present.

One should not think about old problems.

One should learn from the mistakes of the past and take decisions in the present.

"Life exists neither in the future nor in the past. Life is there in the moment you are living now."

-Srimad Bhagavad Gita

According to the Shrimad Bhagavad Gita, life exists in the present, so forgetting the past and giving up worrying about the future, one should live in the present.

"Neither do you think of the past nor worry about the future; focus your mind on the present."

-Gautam Buddha

Lord Gautam Buddha, the founder of Buddhism, has also asked us to focus our minds on the present; there is no use thinking about the past or worrying about the future.

There are three phases of time- past, present and future- in the life of every human being.

1. Past is the time that has passed, the life or time you have lived. As the present of today is the past for tomorrow.

2. The time of today is present, and the time to come is your future.

3. I believe that every human being should live in the present.

4. The efforts made in the present bring satisfying results for the

future.

5. I have found that many people keep thinking about their old problems or troubles, remember the old times, and keep old memories safe in their minds, such as"you had not helped me at that time", "earlier, we suffered a lot", "we have seen awful days, then no one was with us." Things like these keep a person lost in the maze of the past forever.

In the present, if one does not want to live a good life, even after being prosperous enough to afford a decent lifestyle, and keeps clinging to the same old life, then the immediate family feels the pain. Instead of living in the present, that person remains lost only in the past.

Some people think only about the future, accumulate wealth, do not eat well in the present, do not wear good clothes and do not even educate their children well; they only think about how much money they should heap, and if ever someone asks them why they are hoarding wealth, their standard reply is that this money will be useful for them in the future.

Let me share one such incident with you:

An acquaintance of mine was a bank employee but stingy. That person was too miserly in everything, never ate well, wore nice clothes, or even dressed his kids well. To save a few hundred, he used to stitch his children's clothes himself at home, get their hair cut once in three months and sometimes once in six months and wear torn shoes too. When asked why he lived a life of poverty, he used to say that it is just a body; it hardly makes any difference; however, you may wear it. He had lots of money, yet he was lost in his past and let the same environment prevail in his family, due to which the family atmosphere became vitiated, and the whole family could not enjoy the present. Living a penurious life, he happened to pass away one day.

The late bank employee has two sons; the younger one works in a good company abroad in a good position, while the elder one works as a government medical practitioner in India. The elder son had already refused to take a share in his father's property because when he was doing his medical course, his father would refuse to give him money. Even if he gave, it was after a lot of haggling, almost leaving him in tears every time. He could complete his degree in medicine after a lot of struggle.

That boy always thought that my father did not give me money when I needed it. Now that I have everything, what will I do with his property? So he wanted his share of his father's property to be given to the younger brother. And he had also said to his father once that"one day, even your younger son may not accept your property."

That bank employee's doctor son educated the younger brother and sent him abroad for higher education. Later, he got a job, and thus the younger son started living abroad. When he returned home after his father's death, he discovered how frivolously his father had been heaping money for him. He found that even to date, there was a heap of cash, including the notes of one rupee to two thousand rupees. There was a sum of about ₹20 lakhs in the account. He also had some plots of land; the bank employee allocated ₹14 lakhs in such a way that ₹5 lakhs were to be spent on the son's marriage, out of which gold jewellery worth ₹4 lakhs was to be purchased, which would be useful in future. The marriage was to be solemnized on a tight budget of ₹1 lakh. If the son came back from abroad and he did not earn anything, then there was a provision worth ₹6 lakhs, out of which he would be able to live for five years, spending ₹10 thousand per month, and he had even arranged clothes for his son that would last for three to four years.

The cloth arrangement included about eight pairs of trousers-shirts, which he had gifted for his wedding. The pieces of clothing were marked with the year in which they had to be stitched. Every year on the occasion of the new year, a pair of pant shirts was to get stitched. His father had done several things for his son before departing for his heavenly abode. He had written 2-3 letters addressing to his son about the so-called sensible use of the property before he died.

When both the sons saw these things in such a way, they realized that due to this way of their father, the family could not enjoy a good life despite having money. They donated all the properties to the orphanage in their father's name to inspire society.

Both sons had a deep respect for their parents, and were very cultured. If they wanted, they could have hidden their father's deepest and most awkward secret, but the whole family thought that if their revelation could make a few other families learn a lesson about living a good life, then there would be nothing better than that. That's why they set the correct example before the world so that other people could learn from their father's mistake of being embroiled in the past, ruining his present, living a penurious life and leaving it all for the future.

Those who live in the present live well, eat well, and take good care of their family while keeping themselves healthy. They create a happy environment in their family; regardless of the availability of money – less or more – in the household, everyone enjoys the present happily. One should always learn from the mistakes made in the past and improve the present so that there may be pleasing results in the future.

Practice

The real joy of life lies in the present.

Can you be happy in the present, thinking about the future?

Write down moments of happy times of which you have good memories and moments that you could not live.

----

6. One should do the right thing at the right age

Nature has fixed the age of every work.

If one makes a mistake, it should be corrected in time.

Every stage of life should be enjoyed.

Never wait for the right time to come; life is passing many times faster than you think. So do the right thing at the right time.

One should always work according to the age, taking the right decision at the right age. I have seen that people often make decisions irrespective of age, and later they regret it. I have found some people who say that it has become a trend among today's young generation to prefer to take important decisions only after completing a certain task. Still, while doing so, they forget that something for which they are not taking important decisions in their life, the same decisions change their whole life because time waits for none.

There are many such examples:

As some people keep studying till old age, they give birth to children in old age. They indulge in love affairs in their old age. At the same time, some get married in childhood. Some people raise children at the age of grandfather, and some do their grandfather's work in childhood. Just think to yourself whether it seems right.

Relevant work seems appropriate at the right age, so nature has also prescribed age for every work according to which one should act so that one can discharge one's responsibilities well in society and deserve prestige.

Here I would like give two examples to show how one makes mistakes unintentionally and time flies:

First Example:

A close friend of mine was preparing for the UPSC (Civil Service Examination). He is very intelligent. He thought he would only get married once he cleared the UPSC.

Actually, my friend used to think that getting married would disturb his studies. Since my friend's father was posted in a high position in the government service, his father dreamed that his son should become an IAS/IPS officer or get a similarly high rank in the exams. He could barely realize how time slipped while fulfilling his father's dream, and even after putting in his best effort, he couldn't make it. After crossing the UPSC's upper age limit, he again started preparing for MPPSC. He also cleared the Prelims and Mains umpteen times but couldn't make the final cut. Similarly, while preparing for MPPSC, he turned 45.

It was at this age that he decided to get married. He is a good person with a sound family background, so he got married, and he is enjoying a happy married life now. Still, I would say that everything has an age limit, and it is entirely unnecessary to compromise on the important things in one's life or put them on hold merely to achieve a certain goal.

Second Example:

There is a lady doctor in my acquaintance. She is an amiable person. She fulfills all her responsibilities well. In her youth, she believed that getting married would result in an unnecessary increase in domestic duties and burdened by the load; one cannot enjoy one's personal life. She chose to remain single, focus on her career in medicine, and support her family instead. And her life was going on well. She was single and in no mood to give matrimony a chance. She vehemently refused marriage proposals and had no qualms about being a spinster.

Once it happened, while serving food, her nephew's wife told her that she had to cook for bua (father's sister) daily because she came over to have her meals here. It pained the doctor, and she was hurt. She started getting her food prepared at her own home. Time flew by, and she was 50 years old, with no family to call her own and to live a lonely life.

Her health suffered, but there was none to take care of her. The cook used to leave after preparing food, and the servant after doing his work. She used to stay alone at home in the mornings and evenings without anyone around whom she could talk her heart out. The loneliness started getting the better of her, and slowly and steadily, it became a bane for her. Unable to bear the pangs of forlornness, she felt like tying the knot, only to have a companion to whom she could talk and share her feelings of joy and misery. Since she was above 55, she couldn't find a match. Today she is living her life alone. Now, all the time, she needs someone's support to live.

The difference between these two examples is that in the first example, a person made a mistake, but he got an opportunity to correct his mistake, even if not at the right time. He eventually managed to get married. In the second example, a person had no choice but to live a lonely life because she decided to let go of many good marriage proposals at the right time. When she realized her mistake, it was already too late to make a course correction. A person should do the right thing at the right time.

Even if the right time happens to slip by mistake, nature does give a second chance. One should not let the second opportunity slip away; otherwise, one has to repent later. Therefore, one should enjoy every stage of life by doing the right thing at the right time.

Practice

Make a list of the advantages of doing the right thing at the right age and the disadvantages of not doing the right thing at the right age.

----

7. Joy and sorrow

Not only joy but also sorrow should be enjoyed.

Joy and sorrow are like a pair.

One should maintain patience even in bad times.

Time is good or bad, but it definitely passes.

"Do not judge me by my successes. Judge me by how many times I fell and got back up again."

-Nelson Mandela

Everyone in the world always aspires to be happy and prays that no sorrow should ever come into their lives, but it does not happen. In the true sense, the definition of happiness is meaningful only when there has been misery in a person's life because just as a man with a full stomach cannot enjoy food, in the same way, unless there is suffering in a person's life, he can't enjoy happiness.

Just as day and night have a pair, joy and sorrow also have their own. How would it be if there were either day or night only? Just as day and night complement each other, joy and sorrow are complementary to each other. Any person born on this earth could not be an exception to this. Even God himself could not escape from this. None is there who may not have to face sorrow, be it great kings or emperors or sages and saints or leaders or actors or big businessmen, among others.

No one is immune from sorrow.

When the time is favourable, every person should help his people, he should make good memories so that when his bad time comes, he can pass it with the help of his good memories.

When a bad time comes, he does not have to ask anyone for help, but so many people should come to him themselves to offer the help he never expected.

One should always maintain patience in bad times because bad times also pass and are followed by good times. In adversity, we should be happy, thinking that good times are around the corner and will come, and this time will teach us something.

Let me give an example:

I developed a stone at 28, and even after many medicines, when the ailment was not cured, I learned that the stone could be operated out by laser. I had heard that it is a minor operation of hardly 15 minutes, and the patient is discharged on the same day. I thought that since it is such a simple operation, I would get it done in Bhopal. When I went ahead, I was admitted a day before the surgery. I was operated upon to remove that stone. The operation was only for 15 minutes, but after two hours of the operation, when I regained consciousness, I was writhing in unbearable pain. Doctors, nurses, and some family members were standing around me. I realized that I had undergone the operation.

When the doctor asked me how I felt, I smiled, despite the unbearable pain and said, "Well done, doctor!" Everyone was amazed at my response. How can a person say well done in so much pain; I could say so because I knew that this time would pass after a few days, and then the good time will come. I remembered my good days at that time of crisis, rewinding good memories and repeating to myself that this too shall pass, and soon.

When there comes sorrow in a person's life, it hardly goes without teaching him something, or we can say, in such adversity, you try to do your best. Therefore, even when there is a phase of joyfulness, you must be ready that some adverse times may also be lurking around and may come quite unannounced. Thus, if you are prepared in advance, you show patience in times of sorrow, which boosts your family's morale.

One should enjoy both good and bad times because both will pass in no time. So joy and sorrow come in everyone's life, and the person who learns to smile in adversity or keep his chin up in sorrow, no power in the world can make him unhappy, so he should always be happy and enjoy both joy and sorrow.

Practice

You have had both joy and sorrow in your life. You will find the sorrow must have been followed by joy, and the joy must have been followed by sorrow.

Mention your joy and sorrow.

You have finished and arrow in your life. You will find the anti-number rate been followed by joy and the number have their particular value.

8. A successful person

A good person is a successful person.

A good person is good to everyone.

To gain wealth is not to be successful.

Man himself should decide the measure of his success.

"You become as you think."

-Gautam Buddha

Lord Gautam Buddha said that if you think good, you shall become good one day.

"A good mind and a good heart have always been a winning pair."

-Nelson Mandela

Nelson Mandela, a great leader of the world, has said that to be successful or victorious in life, one should keep his mind and heart hale and hearty.

Nowadays, success is measured by the scale of wealth, grandeur and high living of a person. People make big mistakes and do not know that to become a successful person, it is not necessary to have a lot of money, position, wealth, etc., instead, it is enough to be good to be a successful person because a good person has all the qualities that a successful person should have.

A good person, whether a boy or a girl, is good for himself /herself, his/her family, society, the country and the entire human race.

If a good person is a man, then he proves to be a good son, a good brother, a good husband, a good friend and a good father.

That is, he is good for everyone.

Similarly, if a good person is a woman, then she proves to be a good daughter, a good sister, a good wife and a good mother, and she acts as a graceful woman for society.

A successful man does not own riches, a big name, a big position, luxuries, etc.

Happiness always prevails in the family of a good person, the family always stays united. A good person shares every small or big happiness or trouble, success or failure, etc., with his family members.

A good person scales the height of success while discharging his duties and becomes successful.

What is the parameter of success that the person himself should decide?

I put a real-life example before you, and then you decide who you would call a successful person or a good family.

Example:

In a family, there are two brothers- one is a minister, and the other is a big businessman. The family owns a lot of wealth, status, and everything, but there is no unity. In the family, both brothers are jealous of each other. They both have no time for each other. Be it festivals, marriages or any functions, or whenever big parties are organized, the family members never get together to celebrate the occasion. Would you call such a family a successful family?

On the other hand, there is another family where two brothers live together. They do odd jobs, but they have a common kitchen where they cook food for the entire family, and all of them, including small children and old ones, dine together. At a festival or any function, brothers, their wives and children sit together and enjoy the occasion in each other's company. They enjoy their life and never have any complaints against anyone.

Now you have to decide who you consider to be a successful family. I believe success is achieved by being a good person among loved ones. The success achieved by losing the good is worse than the failure. It is better to fail than to achieve success by losing the good.

However many achievements you may have, you will always need a good person.

One who loses his trust is more foolish than one who believes him because he loses a good person forever for his little gain. So don't lose a good person at any cost because a good person is no less than any wealth.

Practice

Who do you consider a successful person?

Are you a successful person?

---

9. Who is to be chosen as a guide or guru?

Who is a guide?

Why is a guide important?

Who do people usually make a guide?

Who should be the guide?

"The teacher is not the one who stuffs the student's mind with facts, but the real teacher prepares him for the challenges of tomorrow."

-Dr. Sarvepalli Radhakrishnan

Every human needs a good guide or a competent guru to lead a good life. This guide can be a parent, brother, sister, friend, relative or any other family member, an outsider, or even your well-wisher.

In childhood, parents often act as a guide for us, but in growing up, a person makes his guide according to his convenience. Still, some people need to learn more about the guide, who is a guide, and why it is necessary to make a guide.

Important information about the guide-

1 Who is a guide?

2 Why is a guide necessary?

3 Who do people usually make a guide?

4 Who should be made a guide?

1. Who is a guide?

A guide or guru is one who, instead of giving you bookish knowledge, gives you proper advice in times of adversity, and helps you solve your troubles and problems, thus making your life happy.

2. Why is a guide necessary?

Everyone needs a good guide every moment to lead a good life because everyone cannot understand everything. Only a few people know how to handle every situation well and spend their life well.

3. Who do people usually make a guide?

It is usually found that a person chooses someone as a guide, one from whom he is most influenced.

4. Who should be made a guide?

A good human being should be made a guide or guru. I can't emphasise enough that a good person is good to everyone.

If ever you want to make a guide, then first of all, you have to ensure that the person you are going to make your guru or guide should be a good person and have a happy family life. In today's environment, around 90% of families have problems. Thus, you must choose the person as a guru or guide from among the remaining 10% of people. Moreover, he should be good for himself, his family, and society. He should be happy, satisfied and have good experiences in life. Such people know the solution to your every problem; only that person should be made a guide or guru.

Example from Mahabharata:

You all do know about the epic Mahabharata. When the war between the Kauravas and the Pandavas was decided in the Mahabharata, both sides went to Lord Krishna to seek his help to win the war. Lord Shri Krishna listened to both sides and said that for me, both of you are equal, so I cannot support either, and my religion also does not permit me to do so.

Lord Shri Krishna told both sides that on one side, I would remain alone without any weapon and would not participate in the war; on the other side, there would be my Narayani Sena. Ask for whatever you want out of the two.

1. Duryodhana was too clever, so he immediately asked Lord Krishna's Narayani Sena. He wondered what Lord Shri Krishna would be able to do all alone without weapons, so he asked Lord Shri Krishna's Narayani Sena, consisting of extraordinarily great warriors excelling one another and millions of soldiers, among others.

2. There, on the other hand, Arjun asked Lord Krishna for his side. Duryodhana lost the war of Mahabharata when he chose only numbers instead of a competent guru.

Lord Krishna was with Arjuna while he gave his Narayani Sena to Duryodhana. Even though Lord Shri Krishna might not have taken up weapons directly in the war, he might not have fought with the Kauravas. Still, he was always with Arjuna (Pandavas) directly or indirectly in every situation.

Lord Krishna had a solution to every problem of the Pandavas. Due to his proper advice and skilful guidance, Arjuna (Pandavas) won the Dharma Yuddha, and Duryodhana (Kauravas) was defeated. The warriors of excelling qualities were fighting on Duryodhana's side, but he did not have any veteran and competent guide or guru like Lord Shri Krishna.

People make the same mistake in real life; they leave their well-wishers for a little benefit, give importance to numbers like Duryodhana did, and ultimately fail in life, so every person should always have his/her good guide with him/her. It should be kept because a good guide stands by you in every situation, and even though he may not be able to help financially, he has the solution to all your problems.

Consequences of not having the right guru or guide:

My wife (Sanyokita Rajput) always dreamed of becoming an IAS because my wife's elder grandfather was a collector, so she also dreamt of becoming a collector. After completing her engineering studies, Sanyokita wanted to go to Delhi to prepare for UPSC. But as all the parents are worried about their children thinking there would be problems in Delhi, they asked her to stay in Bhopal and pursue coaching.

Sanyokita appeared in the MPPSC exams in 2012, 2013, 2014 and 2015 but did not even qualify in the Prelims. It could have happened either because she did not get the right guidance or she had made silly mistakes in the exams.

When I met Sanyokita and saw her hard work, I thought she would be selected if she cleared her Prelims.

Sanyokita qualified for the Prelims in MPPSC 2016 in one go, with little guidance from me. She qualified for the Mains, got good marks in the interview, and was selected for Child Development Project Officer in MPPSC 2016. Later, she qualified for the Prelims, Mains and Interview in MPPSC 2017, which was the result of only proper guidance.

You can see there was hardly any lag in studies, preparation, or dedication. Sanyokita only needed proper guidance, and her dreams got wings.

Usually, people accept a certain successful person as their guide or guru. This successful person may be a good leader, an actor, a good officer, a good scientist, a businessman, a doctor, an engineer, a writer, a journalist, a painter, a good player, or a good poet, among others. Each of these people no doubt happens to have achievements based on their talent in a chosen field, but mostly it is seen that a majority of these people remain in trouble in their real life. On the other hand, some people may not have great achievements or may not be able to do very well in any one field, yet they are the masters of real life, having solutions to all the problems cropping up in life. Only such people are suitable to be accepted as a guide or a guru.

If you see, you will find that there may not be a person who is gifted with all the talents, such as when someone can not become a doctor, an engineer, a scientist, a leader, an actor, a writer, a journalist, etc. But what is common among all of them is that everyone has to live life and wants to live a good life. That's why no matter how big an achievement a person may have, he/she will always need a master of real life, and in real life, a person makes the same mistake with himself or with his family.

Everyone does not know everything. If a person is a great actor, it does not mean that whatever decision he takes will be the right one.

A good guide is a good person who is good to everyone, even if he may not be rich with money but has the solution to all your problems.

As a guide or guru, only those who are good human beings in

real life should be accepted, as their company makes your life very beautiful. We should always keep such people with us, and even if we may have to make some investment in this regard, we should do so.

Practice

Who is your guru or guide?

Does he know the solution to all your problems?

----

10. Marriage

What is marriage?

Who should marry?

Who should not get married?

What is the effect of marriage on success?

When should you get married?

How to choose a good person for marriage?

How to handle a husband-wife relationship?

My opinion about marriage?

Nowadays, there is a lot of confusion among the youth about marriage. In most cases, they cannot decide whether they should get married. There are many advantages of getting married but also some disadvantages. The pros and cons of marriage depend on the person's needs or his own nature.

Who does a person usually marry?

Let us try to understand this through some examples.

In politics, a politician always wants his son or daughter to be married to the family of another powerful politician. An alliance of this kind is desirable because their political hold may be stronger. At times of adversity, some benefits can be sought from another side of the political background. At times, while doing this, they do not even care about the happiness and well-being of their children.

It is seen in Bollywood also that an actor marries another actress or an actress marries an actor. It is okay for an actor to marry an actress, but it is also common for a big actor to marry only a big actress, or a big actress will marry a big actor only. This is so because these people have an issue of prestige or status.

Nowadays, a new trend is in practice. An IAS officer will find a match with another IAS officer only. An IAS officer does not marry any petty officer. If a woman happens to be an IAS officer, then she does not marry an officer below her rank as it becomes an issue of her prestige.

There is a trend in certain societies that our son has a job, and I want a girl with a job too. And if the girl has a job, then the boy should be with a job at any cost; that too, he should be higher in rank and file.

I will give you some examples of where according to me, people make mistakes:

Something common in all the marriages I have discussed above is that some marriages succeed while others fail. The reason is that all these marriages are done apparently to serve their ends, such as, if both big actors and actresses as husband and wife sign a film, then the money they charge will come to their family. Another reason for such a marriage is that if the actor fails, he will have the support of his actress wife, and if the actress fails, then she will support her actor husband. But marriages solemnized for a selfish reason often fails after a certain period. The marriage that is solemnized heartily proves successful.

Bollywood is full of several such examples. Here, giving examples of these people is inappropriate because you all know about such marriages.

Some important points about marriage:

What is marriage?

Who should get married?

Who should not get married?

What is the effect of marriage on success?

When should one get married?

How to choose a good person for marriage?

How to maintain a husband-wife relationship?

My opinion about marriage?

1. What is marriage?

Marriage does not mean becoming husband and wife. Marriage means accepting another person in your life, both positive and negative aspects.

2. Who should get married?

One should not get married on anyone's asking to do so, or as everyone does, so it should be done. Each person knows about themselves and what they are like. They are aware of their positive and negative sides. In my view, every person should marry according to their needs.

Only one should marry who understands that he will need another person in the present or future who may be a husband, wife, son or daughter, among others.

3. Who should not get married?

Those who know that they will not be able to adjust to anyone or will not need any support in the future should not get married. Such people will do as they like and will always expect good from the other person, they will not accept the negative aspects of the other person, or they will not need anyone as a support of their own in future.

For Example:

The positive side of not getting married

Such as

1. For a true ascetic, the whole world is his family.

2. A very big businessman or a person occupying a big position who is supported by many in times of need in future. These people do not have time for marriage or for the family after marriage.

Be it a boy or a girl, everyone has to give time to their partner after marriage. And you don't need to like everything about your partner. There will be some positive and negative things about your partner. One who does not know how to accept the negative side or who does not try to listen or understand the words of one's partner should not get married. Such a person can be happy even by being alone.

4. What is the effect of marriage on success?

Success does not depend on marriage, it depends on one's hard work and self-confidence.

Example:

Many such celebrities worldwide have succeeded by getting married, and many others have succeeded even without getting married.

Successful Married Persons:

1. **Mahatma Gandhi**– One of the world's great leaders with an ideology of non-violence. He is called the Father of the Nation of India.

2. **Abraham Lincoln**– One of the world's great leaders and the 16th President of America.

3. **Bill Gates**– He held the title of the world's richest man for many years.

4. **Sachin Tendulkar**– World famous cricketer who received Bharat Ratna.

5. **Angela Merkel**– German Chancellor (named among the most powerful women in the world).

6. **Karl Marx**– A famous German philosopher.

7. **Roger Federer**– For many years, he held the title of No. 1 Tennis Player in the world.

8. **Vladimir Putin**– He has been the President of Russia for many years, one of the most powerful persons in the world.

9. **Mukesh Ambani**– The richest man in India for many years.

10. **M.C. Mary Kom**– She won the title of world No. 1 female boxer.

Successful Unmarried Persons:

1. **Dr. APJ Abdul Kalam**– A renowned scientist who became the President of India. He was conferred the Bharat Ratna.

2. **Mother Teresa**– A recipient of Bharat Ratna, she was a great social worker in the world.

3. **Ratan Tata**– A noted Indian industrialist.

4. **Queen Elizabeth I**– The Queen of England who was renowned in the world as the Virgin Queen.

5. **Isaac Newton**– He was a famous physicist.

6. **Oprah Winfrey**– Counted among the world's most powerful women.

7. **Lata Mangeshkar**– Known as Swar Kokila.

8. **Leonardo da Vinci**– A renowned painter and sculptor of Italy.

9. **Baba Ramdev**– The great yogi who has carried yoga to every corner of the world.

10. **Atal Bihari Vajpayee**– Former Prime Minister of India and recipient of Bharat Ratna.

5. When to get married?

Be it a boy or a girl, every person should get married at the right time and should do it only by being mature enough to maintain the relationship.

Let me mention one incident.

A gentleman from Bhopal was working in England. He is an intelligent, handsome person with a good job profile, but he was not ready to tie the knot and happened to be almost 40 years of age. He was in a live-in relationship. His parents were badly upset over his refusal to get married. The boy's father lived in my neighbourhood, so he once shared his problem with me. I asked him to introduce me to his son so I could talk with him.

When the boy returned to India, his parents introduced me to him. He did not realize it when I happened to carve out an image of a joyful friend in his heart during a random formal conversation. Instead of advising the boy, I explained it to him by giving a direct practical example, and I was successful.

A Punjabi family lived in my neighbourhood. There was an old mother, and old Sardar Ji lived in the family. The old Sardar Ji had lost his eyesight, and he was hard of hearing too, but that old mother had been serving her husband Sardar for five consecutive years. I told the boy that this woman had not gone anywhere for five years and was only serving her husband while her husband could neither see nor hear. Even after all this, the wife is with her husband. I told him to live as much as possible in a live-in relationship, but this bonding of husband and wife can never be ensured in any such relationship.

One day such a time comes in everybody's life, whether it is wife or husband, but if someone is there to stand by you in old age, it is none other than husband or wife. When you are sick, no matter how much money you spend, hire the best hospital, but no one else can give that feeling of bond that a husband can give to his wife or a wife to her husband.

After this incident, the boy understood that he would also need some partner in the future. Later that boy got married, and today, he is happily married.

6. How to select a good person for marriage?

Every person, whether a boy or a girl, should select a good person for marriage. What happens to the failure of proper selection of the life partner? I am going to explain it by narrating an incident.

An example:

Two of my acquaintances, both of them IAS officers, got married. Both are very intelligent officers. Both were given the designation of the collector. Since there may be only one collector in a district, the government was kind towards them, considering their being husband and wife. It appointed both collectors in the adjoining districts, so their family life remains unaffected due to their official commitments.

The distance between both districts was about 80 km. Usually, the collector has a lot of work, so he/she has to reside at his/her headquarters to discharge his/her official responsibilities very well.

The collector couple was efficiently handling the administration of their respective districts but at the cost of their family life. Both of them could meet once a week or a fortnight. Both of them had a great attitude towards each other. They were hardly ready to listen to each other. Both were adamant about not visiting each other's district– saying, "You come to my district, " and"Why should I come to your district?"

Finally, instead of visiting each other's homes, they would meet in a hotel located in the adjoining area of both districts. After meeting in the hotel when both parted from each other, the hotel owner would be able to understand that they were not the husband and wife but the collectors of the two districts. Because when they left the room, the broken glasses, plates and sometimes even T.V. set would be found broken.

Through this example, I intend to make you understand where you are making a mistake in real life. A good partner should be selected by looking at the environment of his/her family, his/her behaviour and himself/herself, and not by looking at status or position. It would have been better if they had not got married. Then they would have lived a better life because they hardly needed each other.

You can think that even if the Mr. Collector or Mrs. Collector were not in any position to have respect for each other and had a sense of dedication to each other, it would give them moral support, and they would spend their life happily.

7. How to maintain a spousal relationship?

Some important points to handling spousal relationships:

Both husband and wife should respect each other's feelings.

There should be a sense of dedication towards each other.

Both should give some freedom or personal space to each other.

Husband and wife should stay with a joint family for some days.

There should always be something new in the relationship.

Husband and wife should be best friends.

8. My opinion about marriage:

A person must get married because after a certain time, a person, whether man or woman, needs someone or the other. In the beginning, when a person is young, he does not understand that marriage is necessary. He wants to live his free life. But life is not so brief that it may just pass so easily. Sometimes a person happens to get sick, faces troubles, there come moments of joy and sorrow or one gets old, then there is a need for someone, for both woman or a man, of their own.

Every human being, from the cradle to the grave, needs someone or the other. During the childhood phase, our parents take care of us. They do our upbringing very well. The parents do not let us feel the lack of anything, so most of the time, we do not even realize any problem, however big it may be. It is because there is someone or the other living with us. When we grow up, we begin to do things independently without our parents' support, but as they age, we must take care of them.

When we grow old with age or when we happen to face old age, we do not have our parents with us, or if we have not married, then wife and son/daughter are also not there to support us. Then even small trouble or sorrow appears so heavy to us. This is the time when we need someone. That's why a person should get married.

You must have heard an oft-quoted proverb about marriage.

"The laddoo (sweet dish) of marriage results in regret whether one eats or not."

According to the proverb, it is clear that people regret getting married or not getting married, but a person can be happy even by getting married and without getting married.

Some people regret getting married:

Some people regret getting married, thinking they should not have gotten married. And they always keep thinking about how badly they got trapped or, similarly, the girls think to be in the same boat. The husband and boy are mostly heard saying that their life is spoiled. They taunt themselves by blaming their bad luck to have got such a husband or such a wife. Even after all this, some people get married many times in life.

Some people regret for not getting married:

I wish I was married! I wish I had kids, too, I had someone to look after. But today, no one is with me. Many do not get married in the pursuit of making a career but they will regret it later.

Most of the time, people divorce their life partners (husband and wife) on trivial issues-

In my opinion, if someone doesn't happen to be of your liking, then do not force yourself to stay together but at least respect each other's feelings.

Nowadays, people break the relationship on pretty disputes while such issues are common in the family. Some people create an ego issue, such as a girl who thinks, "I am being suppressed; I am also independent, educated, beautiful! Am I here to get confined in the kitchen, etc.?" They get divorced on trivial issues, but they are forgetful of the feeling of affection latent in them. Howsoever strong a woman becomes, her basic nature cannot change. Therefore, she is called an idol of love and affection.

Similar is the case with boys; when they get married, they usually do not care for their wife and want to restrict her freedom completely. This is what results in controversy. Many boys think that as the wife has come now, she has to cook, clean and serve the family. At the same time, they forget that it is the wife who is getting bothered, and in such cases, most of the time, they happen to like another girl, while I say that no one else can love you more than your wife, nor can care for you like her.

Marriage is an important aspect of one's life that changes the entire life. I need to write a separate book to discuss this topic in detail. In that book, both marriage and goal will be elaborated extensively. Marriage and goal are both aspects which influence the life of a person in its entirety.

Let me give you another example:

After clearing the UPSC exam, a girl becomes an IPS. Having studied at IIT, a boy works as the CEO of his father's company. Both get married with their families' consent because the boy's family members have chosen a suitable girl for the boy, and the girl's family members have chosen a suitable match for the girl.

After a few days, both of them get divorced, and all the dreams cherished by both the girl and the boy are shattered because these people married only because the girl was very intelligent as she had cleared the IPS exam in the UPSC; thus, the boy thought this girl would have achievements, and she would be his dream girl. Similarly, the girl also had married, thinking that the boy is very intelligent, a software engineer, and earns a lot of money, owns a company. Both used marriage only as their profit game. Later, both were divorced and never thought they were wrong.

Knowingly or unknowingly or in this world of hectic activity, the decision of marriage should be taken according to your own nature and your needs.

Both husband and wife should know their limits. They should not indulge in things the husband or wife does not like at all. It is common in marital relations to know the likes and dislikes of each other. Therefore, always keep in mind the choice of your partner.

Some important facts about marriage:

Only a few people are happy as married or unmarried people.

According to one's own needs, one should decide whether to get married or not.

Some people relate marriage with success; success depends on your thinking and not on marriage.

You can be successful even by getting married or by not getting married.

Practice

Do you need to get married?

If you are married, list your partner's good qualities.

If you are not married, what qualities do you want in your partner?

Tips for life

We have come to live life, not to spend, so every moment should be lived to its fullest.

To be happy, it is not necessary to be successful in life; you can be happy even after failing.

Every human being should always think so and not underestimate himself compared to anybody.

He/She was unique.

He/She is unique.

He/She will be unique.

One should enjoy every phase of life.

It is a good habit of time that does pass.

Always be ready in life.

Prepare for the best and always be ready for the worst.

One should always strive for the best and be ready for any situation.

Success comes from love and risk, provided that risk and love should be calculated.

I have only two goals in my life-

1. To be a good person.

2. To keep me happy and make others happy at every stage of life.

If you want to do an investment, then do it on human beings, lands do not come to shoulder the bier.

Better to eat by begging than by snatching from people.

Live in such a way that every moment may give you the feeling of having lived your whole life.

Promise that-

I was happy.

I am happy.

I will be happy.

One should enjoy both joy and sorrow.

Every person comes with a unique talent in the world, but he wastes it to become like another.

I am one of those lucky people who have seen the era change.

A decision of a person changes his whole life.

Take decisions and prove them true with your efforts.

Do the right thing at the right age.

The real joy of life is in the present.

A person who changes your whole life is none other than you yourself.

A successful person is a good person.

The person who has learned to smile even in his sorrow, no power in the world can make him sad.

After doing any good deed, reward yourself. After doing good, whether big or small, one should reward oneself.

One foolish friend is equal to 100 enemies, if there is a fool at home, then you don't need to make enemies.

One worthy or learned friend is more than 100 rich friends of yours.

There should always be a good person or the right guide with you.

Separation of ours from you is enough for your downfall.

One should make small goals rather than big goals.

Only giving up the company of a good person opens the way to downfall.

Goals should keep changing with time, provided that you have achieved something while changing goals.

Learn to laugh at yourself. The day you learn to laugh at yourself, you will learn to rule the world.

One should do as much good to all as possible in one's good times and be patient in bad times.

Today 90% of families have problems. And wrong decisions cause those problems, whether taken by the old or younger generations.

Being happy is no less than success.

Be happy, success will come on its own.

Everyone smiles when successful, but it is worth praising if you fail and smile.

Being happy is the solution to all problems.

No matter how many achievements you have, you will always need a good person.

One who loses trust is fooled more than one who believes such a person because he loses a good man forever for his little gain.

If there is a prince or princess of your dreams, it is none other than yourself.

Nowadays, everyone invests in land and I do my investment in humans. This is what makes me different from other human beings.

Before loving anyone, a person should love himself. A person who cannot love himself cannot love anyone else.

Before applying the heart, everyone, whether it is a boy or a girl, should put his/her whole mind, but after applying the heart, one should not put his mind again.

You can be happy anytime with a sense of satisfaction.

Sachin (Sach)

THE WRITE ORDER

You Write. We Publish.

To publish your own book, contact us.

We publish poetry collections, short story collections, novellas and novels.

contact@thewriteorder.com

Instagram- thewriteorder

www.facebook.com/thewriteorder